Fact Finde

~ The American Colonies ~

The Delaware Colony

by Muriel L. Dubois

Consultant:
Professor Samuel Hoff
Department of History, Political Science, and Philosophy
Delaware State University
Dover, Delaware

Capstone
press

Mankato, Minnesota

Fact Finders is published by Capstone Press,
151 Good Counsel Drive, P.O. Box 669, Mankato, Minnesota 56002.
www.capstonepress.com

Library of Congress Cataloging-in-Publication Data
Dubois, Muriel L.
    The Delaware colony / by Muriel L. Dubois.
    p. cm. — (Fact Finders. The American colonies)
    ISBN 0-7368-2673-4 (hardcover)
    ISBN 0-7368-6105-X (softcover)
    Includes bibliographical references and index.
    1. Delaware—History—Colonial period, ca. 1600–1775—Juvenile literature. I. Title.
II. Series: American colonies (Capstone Press)
F167.D83 2006
975.1'02—dc22   2005001879

Summary: An introduction to the history, government, economy, resources, and people of the Delaware Colony. Includes maps and charts.

Editorial Credits
Mandy Marx, editor; Jennifer Bergstrom, set designer, illustrator, and book designer; Bobbi J. Dey, book designer; Kelly Garvin, photo researcher/photo editor

Photo Credits
Cover Image: *Landing of the DeVries Colony at Swaanendael* by Stanley Arthurs, Permanent Collection of the University of Delaware

Getty Images Inc./Hulton Archive, 5; Mansell/Time Life Pictures, 26–27
The Granger Collection, New York, 6, 7, 12–13, 15, 18
Library of Congress, 16–17
Mary Evans Picture Library, 10
North Wind Picture Archives, 11, 14, 20–21, 22, 29 (both)

1 2 3 4 5 6 10 09 08 07 06 05

Table of Contents

Chapter 1

Delaware's First People

American Indians were the first people to call the Delaware area home. The largest group in Delaware was the Lenni Lenape. Many people called them the Delaware Indians.

The Lenni Lenape lived in villages of 100 to 200 people. In winter, they lived in long wooden huts called longhouses. During the summer, they lived in small wooden domes called wigwams.

Villages also had huts called sweat lodges. They were used to treat sick people. Cold water and herbs were poured over hot coals to make steam. Breathing the steam and herbs had a healing effect.

The Lenni Lenape hunted and farmed in Delaware for thousands of years before Europeans came.

Daily Life

The Lenni Lenape lived off of the land. In summer, women planted corn, beans, and squash. They also gathered wild nuts and berries. Men fished in local rivers and in the Delaware Bay. During winter, people ate fruits and vegetables, dried from summer's harvest. For meat, men hunted deer, bears, and turkeys.

At one time, the Lenni Lenape traded with European settlers. ▼

European Arrival

The Lenni Lenape used land to survive. When soil was no longer good for farming, they moved. To them, land was not something that could be owned. The Lenni Lenape had no problem sharing land when the European settlers came.

Settlers gave tools and cloth to the Lenni Lenape in exchange for land. The Lenni Lenape saw these things as gifts. But to the settlers, they were payment for their new land. This confusion led to battles between the two groups.

FACT!

Lenni Lenape means "original people" in the Lenni Lenape language.

The Lenni Lenape and European settlers used wampum belts as money. They were strung with beads made of sea shells. ⬇

Chapter 2

Early Settlers

The Dutch were the first Europeans to settle along the Delaware River. In 1631, about 30 Dutch traders started a village called Zwaanendael. This town lasted less than a year. The settlers had a quarrel with the Lenni Lenape that led to fighting. The Lenni Lenape killed the settlers and burned down their village.

Sweden made the next attempt to settle in Delaware. Queen Christina of Sweden sent an explorer named Peter Minuit to claim the area. In 1638, Minuit and his men landed in what is now Delaware. They called their colony New Sweden.

Many countries wanted control of Delaware. Eventually, it became a British colony. Borders were set in 1763. ➡

The Delaware Colony, 1763

PENNSYLVANIA
COLONY

Delaware River

N
W   E
S

Wilmington

New
Castle

Newark

MARYLAND
COLONY

NEW
JERSEY
COLONY

⭐ Dover

*Delaware
Bay*

Legend

Delaware
Colony

Colony border

First European
settlement, 1631

Capital

City

River

DELAWARE
COLONY

Zwaanendael

ATLANTIC
OCEAN

Scale
Miles
0   5   10

0   5   10
Kilometers

Queen Christina sent Peter
Minuit to start a Swedish
colony in North America. ▼

The Swedes built Fort Christina at what is now Wilmington, Delaware. Settlers there grew tobacco. They also traded tools and cloth with the Lenni Lenape for beaver furs. The colonists sold the tobacco and furs to people in Sweden.

Rival Nations

Meanwhile, the Dutch still wanted the land. Henry Hudson had claimed the land for the Dutch in 1609. In 1655, they attacked Fort Christina and took over New Sweden.

The Dutch made the area part of the New Amsterdam Colony. That colony later became New York.

The English also thought Delaware should be theirs. Samuel Argall claimed the area for England in 1610. He named Delaware Bay after Virginia's governor, Lord De La Warr.

In 1664, the English told the Dutch to hand over the area. If the Dutch refused, England would attack. The Dutch knew they couldn't beat England. They gave the colony up without a fight.

In 1682, England's Duke of York gave Delaware to William Penn. Penn made the area part of his colony of Pennsylvania. He called it the Three Lower Counties on the Delaware.

This early map of Delaware was made when Sweden controlled the area.

FACT!

North American colonists shortened "De La Warr" to "Delaware."

Chapter 3

Colonial Life

The Delaware Colony had been ruled by many countries. Because of its many rulers, people from Sweden, Finland, and the Netherlands had settled there. Each group of people brought parts of their **culture** with them.

Settlers' homes showed their different cultures. Swedish and Finnish people built houses like those in their homelands. Their homes were America's first log cabins. Dutch colonial homes had steep roofs with windows in them. The high windows let in light. This style of home is still popular in America.

The Swedes in Delaware lived like they had in Europe. They built log cabins and used Swedish hay drying racks.

Delaware settlers also shaped American Christmas traditions. The Swedish were the first people in America to decorate Christmas trees. The Dutch made Saint Nicholas part of their Christmas festivities.

⬆ Delaware's large bay and fertile land brought trade and farming to the colony.

Life in the Lower Counties

Colonists in Delaware were farmers and traders. Farmers grew wheat, beans, tobacco, oats, and peas. Some also planted fruit trees and raised livestock. Farmers sold their goods to traders. Traders sold goods to Europeans and people in other colonies.

Men and women divided household work. Men built homes, farmed, and hunted. Women cooked and cleaned. They made clothing for their families.

Even young children helped with chores. They weeded gardens and cared for farm animals. Most children did not go to school. Delaware's first teacher arrived in 1658. At that time, the colony had been settled for 20 years.

Families worked together to survive. Everyone had a job to do. ▼

Chapter 4

Work and Trade

By the mid-1700s, wheat was a successful crop in Delaware. Colonists ground wheat to make flour. Soon, a flour industry developed. Many flour mills were built along the Delaware and Brandywine rivers. Wilmington became a major flour milling center.

Delaware's thick forests provided work for colonists as well. Walnut, oak, and cedar trees grew there. Craftsmen built furniture. Coopers used oak to make barrels. Carpenters cut cedar shingles. Colonists also turned wood into paper. Paper mills sprang up along the Brandywine River.

Delaware's Brandywine River was the site of many flour and paper mills in the 1700s.

Finding Workers

Farmers and traders in Delaware often needed workers. They found help in many ways.

Apprentices worked for master craftsmen for free. In return, a craftsman taught an apprentice his skills. After seven years, masters often gave apprentices tools to start their own businesses.

Some people could not afford the trip to America. They came as **indentured servants**. Local settlers paid for the trip. The settler owned the servant until he or she worked off the debt.

◄ Barrel makers learned their skills as apprentices.

Slavery in Delaware

Delaware's first African slave was brought from the Caribbean to Fort Christina in 1639. Many more slaves were brought to Delaware when the Dutch took over in 1655.

By the 1700s, there were more slaves in Delaware than indentured servants. Farmers and traders made more money owning slaves. Indentured servants left after working off their debt. Slaves worked all their lives. Their children also became the property of the owner.

Delaware Colony's Exports

Agricultural Exports

grain

horses

meat

tobacco

Industrial Exports

barrel staves

bread

cloth

flour

iron

Natural Resource Exports

furs

lumber

Chapter 5

Community and Faith

The many changes in Delaware's rulers greatly affected religion in the colony. Most early settlers had been Swedish Lutherans. Later, the Dutch Reformed Church became the official church. Lutherans met in secret during the 10 years of Dutch rule.

When the English took over, Delaware colonists finally had religious freedom. William Penn thought people should have the right to worship as they chose. This freedom brought many people to Delaware. Catholics, Lutherans, and **Mennonites** were among the settlers who came there.

Government

Delaware was officially part of Pennsylvania until the Revolutionary War (1775–1783). Pennsylvania's government was made up of **representatives** from each county. These men wrote laws for the colony.

Delaware was not like the rest of Pennsylvania. It was made up of Swedish, Dutch, and Finnish people. Delaware's representatives often disagreed with the others. Since there were so few of them, Delaware's representatives usually lost.

◀ William Penn ruled Delaware when it was part of Pennsylvania.

In 1701, William Penn allowed the people of Delaware to make their own laws. In 1704, they elected their first assembly. The colonists made their own laws and ruled themselves. The freedom of self-rule brought more settlers to Delaware.

Population Growth of the Delaware Colony

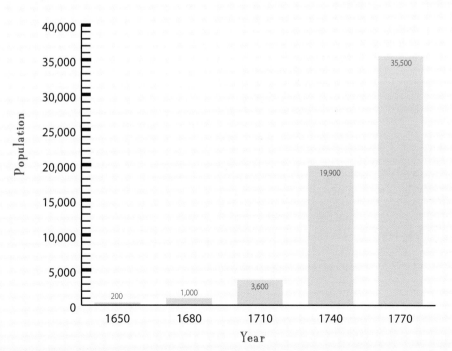

Chapter 6

Becoming a State

Great Britain allowed Delaware self-rule for over 60 years. But in 1763, Britain taxed the colonists on tea, paper, and other items. People in Delaware and the other colonies were torn. Some colonists thought the taxes were unfair, since they had no say in Britain's government. Others remained loyal to Britain.

In 1774, the colonies sent representatives to the Continental Congress. Delaware sent George Read, Thomas McKean, and Caesar Rodney. This group tried to make peace with Britain. But efforts at peace failed. In 1775, the Revolutionary War broke out.

The Proclamation of 1763 set colonial borders. Around this time, Delaware started being seen as a separate colony. ➡

The Thirteen Colonies, 1763

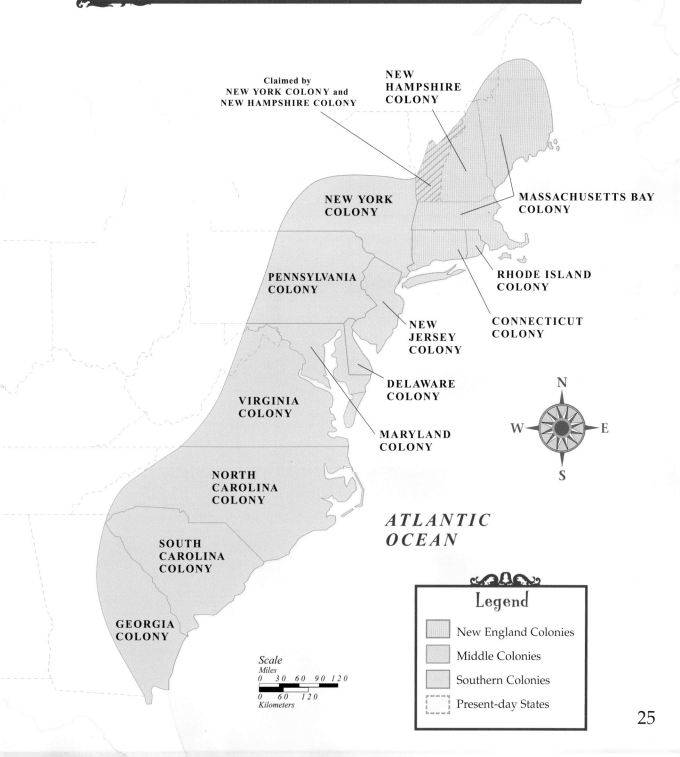

Claimed by
NEW YORK COLONY and
NEW HAMPSHIRE COLONY

NEW HAMPSHIRE COLONY

NEW YORK COLONY

MASSACHUSETTS BAY COLONY

PENNSYLVANIA COLONY

RHODE ISLAND COLONY

CONNECTICUT COLONY

NEW JERSEY COLONY

DELAWARE COLONY

MARYLAND COLONY

VIRGINIA COLONY

NORTH CAROLINA COLONY

ATLANTIC OCEAN

SOUTH CAROLINA COLONY

GEORGIA COLONY

N
W   E
S

Scale
Miles
0   30   60   90 120

0   60   120
Kilometers

Legend

New England Colonies

Middle Colonies

Southern Colonies

Present-day States

Delaware's Hero

The war raged for a year before the Continental Congress voted on declaring **independence**. For the measure to pass, all of the colonies had to agree.

Delaware voted last. Up to that point, every colony had voted for independence. Caesar Rodney was gone that day. McKean wanted independence. Read didn't.

Rodney got word of the vote just in time. Though he was sick, he rode his horse 80 miles (129 kilometers) in a thunderstorm. Exhausted, Rodney arrived just in time to cast the final vote. He voted for independence.

Building a Nation

Congress declared the American colonies free of British rule on July 4, 1776. Delaware leaders wrote a **constitution** later that year. It created the government of the state of Delaware.

After eight years of war, Americans won their freedom in 1783. Four years later, state leaders wrote a plan for a strong central government. It was called the United States Constitution. On December 7, 1787, Delaware became the first state to approve the U.S. Constitution. Today the state's nickname is the First State.

◄ Angry patriots chased British officials out of many Delaware towns.

Fast Facts

Name
The Three Lower Counties
on the Delaware
(1704–1776)

Location
Middle colonies

Year of Founding
1638

First Settlements
Zwaanendael
Fort Christina

Colony's Founders
Dutch traders
Peter Minuit

Religious Faiths
Catholic, Dutch Reformed,
Lutheran, Mennonite

Agricultural Products
Grain, horses, meat, tobacco

Major Industries
Farming, fur trade, lumbering,
manufacturing

Population in 1770
35,500 people

Statehood
December 7, 1787
(1st state)

Time Line

1655
The Dutch take over New Sweden.

1638
Queen Christina of Sweden sends Peter Minuit to begin the colony of New Sweden.

1631
The Dutch start the town of Zwaanendael; it lasts less than a year.

1664
The English take New Sweden from the Dutch.

1682
William Penn makes Delaware part of the colony of Pennsylvania.

1707
An Act of Union unites England, Scotland, and Wales; they become the Kingdom of Great Britain.

1763
Proclamation of 1763 sets colonial borders and provides land for American Indians.

1776
The Declaration of Independence is approved in July.

1775
American colonies begin fight for independence from Great Britain in the Revolutionary War.

1783
America wins Revolutionary War.

1787
On December 7, Delaware is the first state to approve the U.S. Constitution.

Glossary

apprentice (uh-PREN-tiss)—someone who learns a trade or craft by working with a skilled person

constitution (kon-stuh-TOO-shuhn)—the written system of laws in a state or country that state the rights of the people and the powers of the government

culture (KUHL-chur)—the way of life, ideas, customs, and traditions for a group of people

indentured servant (in-DEN-churd SUR-vuhnt)—someone who agrees to work for another person for a certain length of time in exchange for travel expenses, food, or housing

independence (in-di-PEN-duhnt)—being free from the control of other people

Mennonite (MEN-uhn-ite)—a member of a Protestant religion who believes in adult baptism and living a simple, peaceful life

representative (rep-ri-ZEN-tuh-tiv)—someone who is chosen to speak or act for others

Internet Sites

FactHound offers a safe, fun way to find Internet sites related to this book. All of the sites on FactHound have been researched by our staff.

Here's how:

1. Visit *www.facthound.com*
2. Type in this special code **0736826734** for age-appropriate sites. Or enter a search word related to this book for a more general search.
3. Click on the **Fetch It** button.

FactHound will fetch the best sites for you!

Read More

Blashfield, Jean F. *The Delaware Colony.* Our Thirteen Colonies. Chanhassen, Minn.: Child's World, 2004.

Miller, Brandon Marie. *Declaring Independence: Life During the American Revolution.* People's History. Minneapolis: Lerner, 2005.

Whitehurst, Susan. *The Colony of Delaware.* The Library of The Thirteen Colonies and The Lost Colony. New York: PowerKids Press, 2000.

Index